Contents

What are eyes?

eye

Why do animals have eyes?

Animals use their eyes to see.

Where are animals' eyes?

Animals' eyes are on
their heads.

This is a gorilla.
It has eyes at the front of its head.

This is a zebra.
It has eyes on the
sides of its head.

This is an earthworm.
It has no eyes at all.

Different eyes

Eyes come in many shapes and sizes.

This is an owl.
It has round eyes.

This is a mole.
It has small eyes.

This is a frog. It has bulging eyes.
Can you spot the difference?

This is a leopard.
It has shiny eyes.

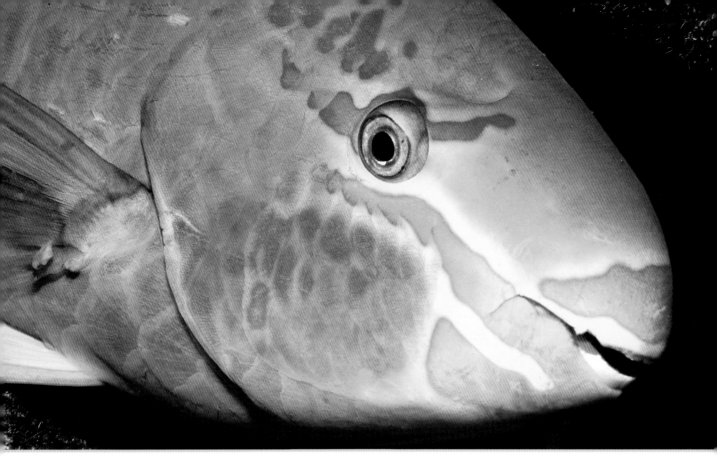

This is a fish.
It has bright yellow eyes.

Amazing eyes

big eye

little eye

This is a bee. It has two big eyes and three little eyes.

This is an eagle.
It can see a tiny mouse
from high up in the air.

stalk

This crab has two stalks on its head.
Its eyes are on the end of the stalks.

This is a chameleon.
Its eyes move separately.
Can you spot the difference?

Your eyes

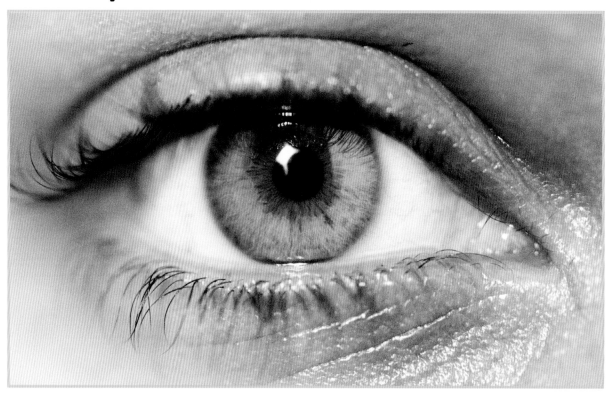

People have eyes, too. Like animals,
people use their eyes to see.

What colour are your eyes?

Can you remember?

Which animal has bulging eyes?
Which animal has eyes on the side of its head?

Picture glossary

 **bright** full of colour

 **bulging** something that sticks out

 **stalk** long, thin "antenna" that some crabs have on their head

Index

Notes to parents and teachers

Before reading

Talk about how we use our eyes to see. Point at things nearby and things far away and ask the child to do the same.

Ask the children to look at friends' eyes. What do they see? Talk about pupils, irises, eyelashes, and the whites of the eyes. Do they think all animals' eyes are the same?

After reading

Play "Hide the coloured wool": Hide strands of different coloured wools at different heights around the room. Give pairs of children one strand and challenge them to find as many matching strands as they can.

Play "Pin the tail on the donkey": Draw a large outline of a donkey (without a tail!) Make a paper tail. Blindfold each child in turn, spin them round once then challenge them to pin the tail on the donkey.